YOU LIFTED MY HEAD

Order this book online at www.trafford.com/07-3045
or email orders@trafford.com

Most Trafford titles are also available at major online book retailers.

Written July 2003

Photography by Michael Gordon.
Cover design by Dzine Konceps.

All Bible verses quoted are from the Authorized King James Version.

Note for Librarians: A cataloguing record for this book is available from Library and Archives Canada at www.collectionscanada.ca/amicus/index-e.html

ISBN: 978-1-4251-6581-9

www.trafford.com

North America & international
toll-free: 1 888 232 4444 (USA & Canada)
phone: 250 383 6864 • fax: 250 383 6804 • email: info@trafford.com

The United Kingdom & Europe
phone: +44 (0)1865 722 113 • local rate: 0845 230 9601
facsimile: +44 (0)1865 722 868 • email: info.uk@trafford.com

10 9 8 7 6 5 4 3 2

YOU LIFTED MY HEAD

L. Iona Halliman

In all thy ways acknowledge Him
and He shall direct thy paths

CONTENTS

Dedication

God, I dedicate this book to You, to Your glory, and to the building of Your Kingdom. I pray Your anointing on every word. Let Your Holy Spirit hover over all who read it and plant in them an eternal seed of righteousness, that they may spring forth into trees of righteousness, planted by God.

To every child of God who is walking, and will walk, the dark paths laid out in this book, may you find encouragement, healing and rest to your souls as you wait upon the Lord to complete His work in you and restore you.

To all those who do not know our God through a personal relationship with the Lord Jesus Christ, may you find life everlasting as you read the pages of this book.

To my sweet, precious ten year old daughter, who was not with me when I did the first handwritten manuscript of this book, I just want you to know that I thought of you often while I wrote. I had mentioned to you that I was going to write a book, and you asked, "When are you going to start writing your book?" That question kept you on my mind while I wrote. I introduced you to God and taught you to love Him, pray to Him and live for Him, from an early age. I am sure that someday you will read "Mommy's book," and as you do, may the God of your childhood, your future and your eternity reveal Himself personally to you and lead you into an everlasting relationship with Him. You are God's child; I dedicated you to Him from before I knew you.

To the army of you who prayed with and for me and wept with me and encouraged me, and did not fully understand what I was going through because you had never been there, and sometimes did not even know what to tell me, I just want to say I love you and I thank you. You made yourselves available for God to use you to help walk me through. Sometimes I did not know what I would do without you. Ultimately, all we need is God, but sometimes we can find Him only in the people He works through. May His blessings overtake you as His goodness and mercy follow you all the days of your life.

Acknowledgement

Thanks to:

Julia Tan who read the manuscript from the perspective of an editor, and passed my attempt at writing as being very good. The fact that you read the entire manuscript in one morning said a lot. I do believe it was God who led me to take occupancy of a house where a Christian editor resided, just one month before He moved upon me to write the book. I do also share your belief that God brought me to you in answer to the desire of your heart concerning Him. This is just a beautiful example of how God in His great providence brings the right set of people together to accomplish His purpose.

My sister-in-law, Jean Fay Halliman-Gardner, who kindly consented to read the manuscript and helped me to search the scriptures for referenced Bible verses. When you passed the manuscript, with suggestions for very minor changes, I knew I was well on my way to becoming a published author. Your vote of confidence in my work meant so much to me. Thank you also for being one of the most understanding, supportive, and encouraging allies in the darkest and most painful period of my life. You have been like a sister from my own mother's womb.

Mrs. sweet, precious Maxine Wright who made herself available to me and counselled me every time I needed her. I will never forget that day at the apartment when I was sinking and I called you, and you rushed to me and prayed for, counselled, and cried with me for four hours. Do you remember how perfectly painful those days were? God is so good. Thanks also to Ronald to whom you introduced me. Ronald, thanks for the times you spent with me on the telephone, counselling me and helping me to understand some of what I was going through from a psychological and a male point of view.

My sister, Mrs. Janet Wright, with whom I spent hours on the telephone weeping and praying. You tried to assure me more than anyone else of God's forgiveness. Your labour was not in vain.

My daughter who was such a darling to me through it all. The love, the care, the prayers, the special little favours, the little attempts at reconciliation between Mommy and Daddy, the tears you cried with me, the song you made up and sang to me each morning: "Mommy, Mommy, Mommy, Mommy is pretty today" (repeat x infinity). Sometimes you "sent me up the gum tree" with your song, but at times I found it so funny I would just smile, and occasionally, I even caught it repeating itself away in my heart. At times you were harsh with me, thinking that this approach would cause me to turn my life around. Mommy loves you -- always.

My precious Mom, Isolyn Ebanks, who understood so well the things I wanted to hide from her because I feared she would not understand, or accept that her Christian child had done what she did and had come to such a dark place in her life. Mother, you never condemned me, but you assured me of your love and God's love, and you assured me of God's total forgiveness. Your understanding and acceptance helped me to overcome. The very same thing goes for my sister Julian Mills and my brother Derron Ebanks. Above all Mom, I thank you for a Godly heritage.

Special thanks to my employers who supported me morally and financially, and put up with all the mess that I was and all the mess I created on the job. So many times I wanted to go through the door voluntarily before you sent me, and so many times your patience and your tolerance wore thin, and you still extended yourselves.

Thanks also to my co-workers, who were all so understanding and supportive.

Thanks to all the others of you -- you know yourselves -- who contributed in even the minutest way to my healing and restoration. I could write another book just acknowledging you individually.

Above all, I thank God for His inspiration to write this book. Although the desire to write was implanted in me three years before, and the content and purpose of the book would have taken a different course if there had been a reconciliation of my marriage then, as I had expected, the anointing to write this book never came until July 2003, and almost the entire book was handwritten, typed, and about the first three drafts done, all in the first two weeks of July. This shows me that when God calls, inspires, and anoints -- anything can be accomplished by anyone He chooses, as long as that one submits himself to God.

PREFACE

God inspired me to write a book out of the ashes, pain, mourning, fear and despair which resulted from my broken marriage. Being in the seventh month of separation from my husband, God changed my heart after He had brought me to the point of surrender to Him concerning returning to my matrimonial home. Before surrendering my will to God, I had no desire at all to return, I only just wanted a divorce. But immediately (overnight, literally) after praying and handing the situation over to Him, He changed my heart, and divorce was no longer an option for me. I prayed to God on Wednesday night filled with anger, bitterness and resentment towards my husband, and I awoke on Thursday morning in love with him and ready to go home. Ironically, it was on that very day that my world was turned up side down, as I had a revelation of something that shattered my life -- just when I thought I would have my marriage back, I discovered that it was out of my reach. Subsequently, each of several attempts made to reclaim it proved futile, until I concluded that it was out of my hands and at a place where ONLY God could restore it.

What ensued gave birth to my story, which tells of the magnitude of pain and depression I subsequently suffered, the sin I fell into, and God's great faithfulness and grace through it all. This book gives an account of that very dark period of my life. It is not meant to be a detailed account of my matrimonial experiences, but it sufficiently covers the main purposes for which it was written, namely, to testify of God's faithfulness in the worst deal that life handed me, and to encourage, comfort and strengthen anyone and everyone of like affliction.

There are many failed marriages all around, and having set out on a small mission to understand men, and having come to some amount of understanding of how different the sexes are, I believe one of the causes of failure is a basic misunderstanding spouses have of each other. We are truly engineered differently, and I can see where my own marriage might have failed because certain behaviours on the part of my spouse, which I perceived to be characteristic of him, were in fact behaviours that can reasonably be expected of men in general. Some of these behaviours result from the way in which men were socialized and what they perceive society expects of them.

For example, there was a time when I considered my spouse to be hard, cold, selfish, inconsiderate, and insensitive, and I saw those behaviours as weapons being used against me. I did not expect this from someone who meant so much to me and to whom I thought I meant so much. I intensely protested those behaviours. My mission to understand men led me to discover that these are common perceptions that women have of their men, and most times men have no idea what we are talking about when we accuse them of those undesirable qualities. On a point of clarity, I am not saying that I am now ready to accept any kind of treatment from any man; I believe sometimes we all have to curb our natural tendencies for the sake of good relationships, especially marital ones.

While I do not assume total blame for the failure of my marriage, I acknowledge that my response to the perceived undesirable qualities in my husband did play a great role in its disintegration. In retrospect, I can fully appreciate the need my husband must have felt to find companionship elsewhere. While I do not condone his action, I open myself to understanding, especially since I, too, felt the need to turn to someone else for consolation from the pain I felt in the marriage.

I hasten to say that despite whatever went wrong in my marriage, the union brought many beautiful, wonderful, special moments into my life, moments which will always hold a special place in my heart, and moments for which I am joyfully grateful.

Verses

Thou hast turned for me my mourning into dancing: Thou hast put off my sackcloth, and girded me with gladness; To the end that my glory may sing praise to Thee, and not be silent. O Lord my God, I will give thanks unto Thee for ever.

Psalm 30:10-11

To appoint unto them that mourn in Zion, to give unto them beauty for ashes, the oil of joy for mourning, the garment of praise for the spirit of heaviness; that they might be called trees of righteousness, the planting of the LORD, that He might be glorified.

Isaiah 61:3

But Thou O Lord art a shield for me, my glory and the lifter of my head.

Psalm 3:3

CHAPTER 1

SIN AND SEPARATION

That night, I had a dream in which Jesus and I were walking in a cornfield somewhere in St. Elizabeth.

ISAIAH
CHAPTER 59:1-2

Behold, the Lord's hand is not shortened, that it cannot save; neither His ear heavy, that it cannot hear: But your iniquities have separated between you and your God, and your sins have hid His face from you, that He will not hear.

WHEN the Spirit of man abides in the presence of God, this is life, and heaven on earth. When the spirit of man is separated from the presence of God, this is death and hell on earth. What is the great separator from God and His presence? Sin.

I write this book from a Christian perspective. All that this book reveals happened in my walk with Christ. In fact, if it had happened prior to the start of my walk with the Lord, there would not have been an experience to share, because I would never have been able to tell the horror of feeling separated from the presence of God if I had not dwelt in His presence before, for over twenty years.

Those who have never committed their lives to Christ do not know the hell of being separated from Him in this present life. However, for those of us who have been born into the family of God and have diverted from the paths of righteousness into the paths of sin and destruction, we can truly testify that in this life we can afford to lose ALL, as long as we have Christ and the light and life of His presence abiding with us. To experience the abiding presence of God in which there is fullness of joy, is to accept Christ into our lives as Saviour and Lord and to follow, in obedience, in the paths of righteousness in which He leads.

During the time of marital difficulties before leaving my matrimonial home, I shared my deep pain with someone of the opposite sex with whom I was acquainted. He showed sympathy and understanding and over a period of time, a friendship developed between us. Out of this friendship, a relationship of an intimate nature developed. This was not a deep or consistent relationship, because the Spirit of God constrained me, and I just could not find it within myself to be so inclined, but it became deep enough to cause me to fall into adultery. Falling into the sin of adultery as a woman of God took me to a place to which I would never, ever want to return. In my experience, which happened one afternoon as I sat in a secluded office at work consumed by guilt and a great feeling of condemnation, it seemed like I was at the "gate of hell". I never felt the flames of hell, but I distinctly remember experiencing three things that *seemed* worse. These were: (1) utter, suffocating darkness, (2) utter hopelessness, and (3) utter separation from God. It was the last of the three that was most tormenting, and through this experience, I do believe that I can identify even to a very small extent with Christ, when on the cross, bearing **every** sin of the **entire** world, He felt separated from His Father, God, and cried out: "My God, my God, why hast Thou forsaken me?" (Matthew 27:46). What a horror, that God should forsake someone; that someone should be cut off from the presence of God!

This may seem quite a vague representation of that experience, but to me it was so vivid that for over one year, I felt I had lost my salvation. I repented and prayed for forgiveness so many times, but I could not sense God's forgiveness. Because I did not feel forgiven, I constantly doubted and I constantly felt condemned. So many times I asked *His forgiveness* for doubting *His forgiveness* -- talk about a mess! I struggled long with this. I lost everything I had come to experience in my over twenty years of being a Christian -- I lost the awareness of the presence and love of God, I lost my joy, I lost my peace, I lost my blessed assurance, I lost my hope in Christ. In fact, whereas the matter of Christ's return was always a source of pure joy and anticipation, I now dreaded the possibility of His imminent return. All I could feel was a lingering sense of fear and condemnation. I was so convinced that I was lost; that God in His great love for me had given me the gift of eternal life and I had thrown it away because I had foolishly fallen into the sin of adultery.

I tried SO HARD to "find" His presence, and to find again all the fruit of the Spirit which I had once fully enjoyed. I shared with SO MANY people, who prayed for me. I sent e-mails to just about every Christian ministry I could find on the Internet -- those we in Christendom are all more or less familiar with through cable television -- just to get a word of assurance that I had not lost my salvation. I sought long and hard.

One night, after praying specifically for my husband and the one he was "now" involved with, and expressing to God my love and forgiveness for them despite the excruciating pain they had brought into my life, I went to sleep. That night, I had a dream in which Jesus and I were walking in a cornfield somewhere in St. Elizabeth, where I am from. The cornfield was actually in a neighbour's front yard (in the dream). We walked and talked together. We eventually moved to the back yard, where we sat and continued talking. During our conversation, I said to Him, "Lord, please forgive me for that thing." He said to me, "**What thing**?" I responded, "You know Lord." I also told Him that because of it, I felt like I was going to hell. At that point, He took a stenopad (a secretary's notebook) and wrote something in it. He then handed the stenopad to me and told me to sign it. Much was written on it, but the only part I clearly saw was the sentence that read, "You are not going to hell." I signed the page and gave the stenopad back to Him. I also remember that prior to that, He was doing a lot of writing on a separate note pad.

After all this, we walked towards the house, and as we approached, I called out to my parents who were coming outside. I told them that the person with me was Jesus, and of course, they brushed aside that notion. I tried to convince them that it was in fact Jesus, and I turned to Jesus and asked Him to give them a sign. A sign then appeared in heaven. As we looked up, the clouds parted and a portion of heaven was revealed. What an awesome sight that was! The colour was a beautiful bright sky blue, and we saw some sights, which I do not remember clearly. At that point, that portion of heaven descended to a certain level, and then ascended, and the clouds came back together.

When I shared this dream with about six persons and mentioned the part where Jesus asked me, "**What thing**?" everyone's immediate response was, "See, God has forgiven you, He does not even know what you are talking about." Remember, the Word of God says that when we confess our sins to Him and He forgives us, He does not remember our sins anymore. He sees us just as if we never sinned. Oh, how many times I looked back at that dream and drew strength and assurance from it when the "accuser of the brethren" came and laid condemnation on me. God saw how desperately I was struggling to believe He had forgiven me. He saw the lengths to which I had gone, He saw how many people had tried to reassure me, and He saw my continued distress, and so, He had to come to me personally in a dream that I could draw on each time the devil planted doubt and fear in my heart. What a God! He is just so "something else." If you are a child of God, you know how it is when you cannot find the words to express the goodness, the wonder, and the love of God.

What made accepting the truth of God's forgiveness so difficult for me was twofold. In the first case, I perceived the sin of adultery to be so great and shameful, and in the second case, this great sin was committed as a Christian. I found it difficult to forgive myself and I kept beating up on myself, saying things like, "I cannot believe I did that!" and "How could I have done something like that!" I truly could not believe I had done something like that. After all, I had been a Christian for over twenty years, and I was twelve and a half years in marriage; and now, this. My purity in marriage was one of the things I dearly treasured; and now, this. I just could not come to terms with it.

But, follow the story and see the goodness of God unfold.

Come now, and let us reason together, saith the Lord: though your sins be as scarlet, they shall be as white as snow; though they be red like crimson, they shall be as wool.

Isaiah 1:18

CHAPTER 2

I KNOW WHOM I HAVE BELIEVED

I cannot pinpoint exactly when God brought me to that place of peace.

2 TIMOTHY
CHAPTER 1:12

...for I know whom I have believed, and am persuaded that He is able to keep that which I have committed unto Him against that day.

MY quest to find peace with God after my fall ran a course of approximately two and a half years. I cannot pinpoint exactly when God brought me to that place of peace, but it just dawned on me one day that the greatly oppressive heaviness, the fear, and the torment associated with the memory of my sin were no longer constant in my life. This constancy was such that every single day for about two and a half years, this sin rested on my mind. I was living under the shadow of its darkness, and my thinking was that if I had no hope in Christ at the end of this life, then life was totally meaningless, and nothing I did could bring meaning to it. If I had everything -- house, money, car, a fulfilling job, degrees, status, the ability to travel the world, health, a marriage made in heaven -- all this would mean nothing to me, because I could not enjoy or find fulfillment in anything if the Lord Jesus Christ was not a part of my life, and if I could not close my eyes in death with Him by my side.

God used many means by which He brought me to that

place of peace with Him. He reminded me that He is God who cannot lie, and if He had said that He would forgive me of my sins and cleanse me from all unrighteousness if I confessed my sins to Him, then that was exactly what He meant. He reminded me that if I as a human being could forgive my child for whatever wrong she did whenever she did it, how much more He, being God and my Father, would forgive me for *whatever, whenever.* He reminded me that His attributes are limitless, and His willingness and ability to wipe the slate clean are never depleted. And He reminded me of one of my favourite Bible verses of old, (hence one of my favourite hymns), a part of which is the title of this chapter: "For I know whom I have believed and am persuaded that He is able to keep that which I have committed unto Him against that day." My understanding of this verse is that the sins we have confessed and committed to God, can no longer condemn us on the day of judgement. And finally, He appeared to me in a dream as stated in the previous chapter.

Would you believe that until this day the devil still tries from time to time to throw that sin into my face? But when he does, I do not feel guilty anymore, I do not feel heavy anymore, and I do not feel fearful anymore. What I experience now whenever the accuser reminds me of my past, is joy, peace, and assurance, because God defends me and reminds me that He is able to keep that which I have committed unto Him against that day -- He has it well covered under the blood of Jesus.

And they said, Believe on the Lord Jesus Christ, and thou shalt be saved, and thy house.

Acts 16:31

CHAPTER 3

WRESTLING WITH GOD

I had reached a stage in the relationship where I was filled with anger, bitterness, and resentment, and I felt there was absolutely no hope for a workable marriage.

JOB
CHAPTER 40: 1-8

Moreover THE Lord answered Job, and said, Shall he that contendeth with the Almighty instruct Him? He that reproveth God, let him answer it. Then Job answered the Lord, and said, Behold, I am vile; what shall I answer Thee? I will lay mine hand upon my mouth. Once have I spoken; but I will not answer: yea, twice; but I will proceed no further. Then answered the Lord unto Job out of the whirlwind, and said, Gird up thy loins now like a man: I will demand of thee, and declare thou unto me. Wilt thou also disannul my judgement? Wilt thou condemn me, that thou mayest be righteous?

WAS I a rebel, or does it happen to all of us who know God? Do we all wrestle with Him at some point in our walk with Him? I came to experience this wrestling match when I determinedly wanted to end my marriage -- although I knew God's perspective on divorce. But, regardless of God's perspective, I wanted it officially over and done with. I had reached a stage in the relationship where I was filled with anger, bitterness, and resentment, and I felt there was absolutely no hope for a workable marriage.

Thus, my struggle with God began.

How could He honestly expect me to stay in a marriage which was causing me so much emotional pain and unhappiness? And so the struggle continued for the next six months until that particular Wednesday night when I could struggle no longer, and I submitted to God [it is indeed hard to kick against the pricks (Acts 9:5)]. I threw myself across my bed and said to the Lord, "God, You know that I am not willing to go back to my husband, but I know that You hate divorce, and because You hate divorce, I hate it too. Lord, even though I am not willing to go back, I am willing for You to make me willing." During my sleep that night, God transformed me, as I woke up on Thursday morning, in love with my beloved. All the anger, bitterness, and resentment were gone, and I was ready to go home.

My situation did not change, but God changed my heart, and oh, how wonderful it was to be free from all the years of built-up "hatred" towards my husband!

For thus saith the high and lofty one that inhabiteth eternity, whose name is Holy; I dwell in the high and holy place, with him also that is of a contrite and humble spirit, to revive the spirit of the humble, and to revive the heart of the contrite ones.

Isaiah 57:15

CHAPTER 4

I SURRENDER ALL

Even if at first the situation is perturbing, as many situations in our lives will be, I can easily surrender to the fact that God is in control and it is well done.

1 PETER
CHAPTER 5:6

Humble yourselves therefore under the mighty hand of God, that He may exalt you in due time.

I learned through letting go of my struggle with God that surrender to Him brings peace and a wonderful sense of wellbeing. It was an act which allowed God to lead me beside still waters and restore my soul. It also opened the door for me to be blessed and to be used by Him.

This experience taught me to submit every other area of my life to Him on an ongoing basis. I so desire to be submitted to God that I do not want to do anything that even *seems* to be out of His will. Doing His will has become more important to me than my life; and I can testify that His will is not always easy. Sometimes it is hard; very, very hard, and sometimes extremely painful, but ultimately, it is the safest and most rewarding place to be.

The result of surrendering all is that I can now look at everything that happens in my life from a positive perspective. If my all is surrendered to God, then God is in total control. If God is in total control, then I can truly say that whatever betides me, indeed it is well done. It may hurt and cause a lot of pain, but it is well done. It may be totally beyond my human mind to comprehend, but it is well done. I may quarrel with God about it, but it is well done. It may seem senseless, but at the end of the day God's ways are higher than my ways and His thoughts are higher than my thoughts and therefore, it is well done.

This is such a restful place to be. Even if at first the situation is perturbing, as many situations in our lives will be, I can easily surrender to the fact that God is in control and it is well done, and thus find great peace and rest in the midst of the storm.

Take my yoke upon you, and learn of me; for I am meek and lowly in heart: and ye shall find rest unto your souls.

St. Matthew 11:29

CHAPTER 5

GETTING TO KNOW GOD

I did not want to live. I prayed often that God would take my life and I was bombarded by suicidal thoughts.

PHILIPPIANS
CHAPTER 3:10

That I may know Him, and the power of His resurrection, and the fellowship of His sufferings, being made conformable unto His death.

... "THAT I MAY KNOW HIM"...

THERE is a song by a popular local gospel group that I love dearly. It talks about just wanting to know God ***so well***. I often sang that song, and it was always a prayer from my heart when I sang it.

I have learned that the way to truly get to know God is through hardship and suffering. Oh sure, I was a Christian for over twenty years before I experienced real suffering (which I will expand on next). I attended Church regularly, I was involved in several ministries, I knew my Bible fairly well, I developed my relationship with God, I did everything that was expected as a child of God, and I thought I knew everything there was to know about Him, but I was about to enter into the valley of deeper revelation.

... "AND THE POWER OF HIS RESURRECTION" ...

Jesus Christ is the resurrection and the life (St. John 11:25).

There is nothing in our lives so dead that His resurrection power cannot make alive again. My circumstances came under His resurrection power, and as you read along, you will see how He brought many dead situations in my life, back to life. Nothing can remain dead under the resurrection power of the Lord Jesus Christ -- nothing.

... "AND THE FELLOWSHIP OF HIS SUFFERING..."

My suffering started on that fateful Thursday when I woke up and discovered that God had restored my love for my spouse. The ecstasy I felt at the start of the day was short-lived, as my husband turned up at a family gathering (that same day) with someone else by his side. Before I made the connection, I spoke briefly with him, and his eyes sparkled, and of course, I thought they were sparkling for me. However, as time progressed, I started to sense that something was not right in "my paradise." By the end of they day, I was a bundle of pain. It took me only a few days to plunge into the depth of depression, after having dinner with my husband and hearing from him that he was not interested in a reconciliation at that time. He also offered very little hope for reconciliation at a future date; all he kept saying was that I should be positive.

How ironic that re-discovery of love for my husband should have happened at such a time. Why did God allow it? For one thing, this book would not have been written if it had not happened, and all the good that came out of this dramatic situation is the storyline of this book. Sometimes we just cannot see or understand the purposes of God, but we just have to, in faith, accept that His ways are higher than our ways and His thoughts than our thoughts (Isaiah 55:9). We just have to acknowledge that His ways are past finding out (Romans 11:33), and that He is sovereign and in total control of our circumstances.

Well, acceptance of the loss of my marriage slowly dawned, and thus began my period of great suffering. I can only try to express what I have been through, but you will not fully understand unless you have gone through this same valley or you are at present going through it. I went into suicidal depression which continued unabated for over two years. I will share with you some of what I went through as a result of the depression, an affliction which in my estimation is the worst thing that can befall man. This grave depression ran concurrently with the ultimate feeling of loss I experienced in thinking I had lost God also, so imagine the anguish I went through.

I could not eat, and so I went down from 110 pounds to 94.5 pounds. My clothes hung on me like they hang on a clothes hanger. As this was the case, I usually felt so sick and weak. Even with an appetite stimulant, I was able to eat only a very small amount of food, which I had to fight to swallow. My stomach seemed to repulse food, and my throat seemed to lock down whenever I tried to swallow. After several months, I cried out to God to grant me my appetite back so I would not have to take an appetite stimulant daily, in order to eat. God shortly restored my appetite, and I never once had to touch that thing again. I have eaten normally since, and have steadily regained my weight.

I could not sleep, because the depression so tormented me at nights, and the little sleep I got produced nightmares and visions I would rather not have seen. These visions involved my husband and his new friend together, or me being back in the matrimonial home but not quite fitting in. I would always awaken from these dreams in such emotional pain.

I could barely drag myself out of bed in the mornings, because the weight of the depression was so heavy, it crushed me. I felt like I was carrying a ton on my chest. What made it worse was that for over two years, <u>every single day</u>, on awakening from whatever little sleep I got in the wee hours of the morning, my husband was always, always -- always, the first thing on my mind. From the exact instant my eyes opened from sleep, he was present, on my mind.

On occasions too numerous to recall, I felt like I was going crazy. Now, this one I cannot describe. Only God could understand those sensations in my head. I really thought I was going to lose it. My studies came to an abrupt end. I could not read the newspaper, listen to the radio, or watch television. I did not want to hear music of *any kind*, and consider this from someone who considered herself to have music in her bones. All those activities made me feel like I was going crazy. I could not understand what was happening to me.

One night after coming home from a computer class I had "attempted" (rightly so because I was there, basically in body only) I went straight to the telephone and did a three-way call with my sister in St. Elizabeth and my sister-in-law in Kingston, and told them I was afraid because I felt like I was about to lose my mind. I cried uncontrollably throughout the conversation, because I was frightened of what was happening and the sensations in my head were so weird. They talked and prayed with me, and I managed to make it through another night.

On another occasion at about one-thirty in the morning, this feeling was so overwhelming that I had to talk to someone. I did not know whom to call at that time of the morning, but I just had to talk to someone or I felt I would certainly lose my mind if I did not. I eventually mustered the courage to dial the number of someone I had known for about twenty years, but whom I was totally out of touch with except that we had crossed each other's path about a year earlier. The telephone rang several times without an answer, so I hung up. However, I still *had to* talk with someone, so I picked up my cellular telephone and dialled the number of an overseas Christian ministry and briefly explained my desperation. The telephone counsellor encouraged and prayed with me, and I was finally able to go to bed, greatly relieved from the pressure in my head, after crying a little.

I could not read the New Testament of my Bible, because there was always something there to remind me of the adultery I had committed and make my already heavy spirit much heavier. I only read Job, the Psalms, Isaiah, Jeremiah, and a few other Old Testament books. I related this experience to a young man with whom I spoke regularly, who was also going through a marital breakup, and he told me he had a similar difficulty in reading the New Testament. I found great comfort in knowing this was not exclusive to my situation.

I could not function in Church, at home, or at work. Talk about work! That is a story in itself. It was ONLY by the grace and favor of God that I still had my job. I was an embarrassment to myself, and I believe everyone felt the frustration of my performance, which had practically dropped to zero. My employers, however, despite their weariness of me, helped and encouraged me through that great ordeal.

I was washed daily by mighty waves of hopelessness. I felt like "Humpty Dumpty" -- broken, un-whole and "unputbackable." So many times I reached the point where I wanted to give up, because I just did not have the strength spiritually, mentally, emotionally, or physically to carry on, and yet, I had a job that I had to go to and fall apart on every day, and a sweet, precious daughter who had not even yet reached age ten to live for and take care of. I felt like a child myself, who needed someone to take care of me. I was tempted on a few occasions to invite some relative from the country to come and take care of me, for pay.

NOTHING brought me joy or pleasure anymore; I did not want to go *anywhere* or do *anything*. Life is full of many little pleasures, and everyday there is something to enjoy. This, however, was no longer the case for me.

I was just like a restless ocean with irritability, a condition which was almost unbearable. I could not sit or stand still, being constantly fidgety and agitated. Whenever I sat, my hands just kept going, and I could not sit for long before getting up again or moving from one place to another.

I took anti-depression pills, sometimes three per day, almost everyday for well over one year, and while they helped to ease the pain and depression somewhat, they put my life at risk because sometimes on my way to work in the mornings, I would find myself almost falling asleep around the steering wheel, coming too close to someone's car bumper, or almost running off the road onto the sidewalk. But, I just could not function without the pills. I cried out to God and asked Him to take me off them, and He did. Even though I was still deeply depressed, God made me able to function without them.

I lacked energy and had to push and will myself to do *everything*.

My mind lacked clarity and focus, and the simplest

tasks became the greatest tasks, because of the great difficulty I found in doing everything. I learned during my ordeal that such depth of depression can literally dim the eyes, and I had this experience several times even with the wearing of my eyeglasses.

I experienced various nervous conditions, including an involuntary twitching of my lower jaw and grinding teeth (bottom and top rows of teeth tightly clamped together at all times). My jawbones actually hurt and felt tired from that condition.

I felt I would never get out of what I was going through and that this was the longest period of my life.

Tears came easily and unexpectedly, no matter where I was. This sometimes caused great embarrassment, especially when it happened on the job. I often had to run to the restroom so no one would see me cry. My red eyes and nose always "told" on me, though.

I DID NOT WANT TO LIVE. I prayed often that God would take my life and I was bombarded by suicidal thoughts. I never felt a compelling desire to take my life, but the thoughts were my constant companion, and no matter how hard I tried to banish them from my mind, they would not go: (Why not just walk out into the road and let a vehicle hit you down? Why not jump from the balcony? Why not just use the knife you have in your hand and do something? Why was it that person that died and not me?). Such were my running thoughts. Sometimes I wished I could gather them all together and tie them to the bedpost.

My self-esteem and self-confidence took a nosedive, especially on the job, and I kept comparing myself to the other person in my husband's life. I felt she had everything above me, and I felt so small and valueless to my husband.

Groaning became a prayer language for me, because so often when I felt the need to pray, or when the pain was so intense, the only thing I could do was groan. Sometimes when the pain was so unbearable I would hug and squeeze myself tightly and just groan, but the groaning was literally like having a conversation with God.

Imagine living all that, with everything happening at the same time, for almost two years with very insignificant relief. I wept and cried out to God day and night, and through that period of **great** darkness I witnessed His **greater** *faithfulness* like never before. God and I have walked through the fire, through the flood, and through the tempest, and it is my heart's greatest desire to give Him all the glory for this mighty deliverance.

And I will give them an heart to know me, that I am the Lord: and they shall be my people, and I will be their God: for they shall return unto me with their whole heart.

Jeremiah 24:7

CHAPTER 6

SUFFERING AS A SPIRITUAL MIRROR

Sometimes we think more highly of ourselves than we ought, and if God does not bring us face to face with ourselves, we stumble along thinking we are the best thing since creation.

JAMES
CHAPTER 1:22-25

But be ye doers of the word, and not hearers only, deceiving your own selves. For if any be a hearer of the word, and not a doer, he is like unto a man beholding his natural face in a glass: For he beholdeth himself, and goeth his way, and straightway forgetteth what manner of man he was. But whoso looketh into the perfect law of liberty, and continueth therein, he being not a forgetful hearer, but a doer of the word, this man shall be blessed in his deed.

ONE of the things I discovered about suffering as a Christian is that God uses suffering as a mirror to show us ourselves. In the spirit, I found myself standing before this mirror, and I saw myself more clearly than I ever did before. The difference between the natural and the spiritual mirror is that the natural mirror shows the external only, while the spiritual mirror shows both the external and the internal.

Facing myself so openly was such a spiritual exercise. I saw so many things in myself that I was not aware of before and that I was not at all happy with. For example, I never linked the bitterness and anger towards my husband to unforgiveness, and I did not realize that certain behaviours in my marriage could be classified as unsubmissive. You may be thinking at this point that I am one of those wives who "bow" to their husbands. I do not consider myself as such, but I must point out that God dealt very sternly with me concerning the matter of submission during the first year of separation.

Sometimes we think more highly of ourselves than we ought, and if God does not bring us face to face with ourselves, we stumble along thinking we are the best thing since creation and everything about us is the way it ought to be. After beholding myself spiritually, I knew that I needed God to change some things about me, and as He revealed them to me, I presented them to Him. Little by little, He brought about, and continues to bring about change, taking me from glory to glory.

Although I am not yet perfected, because perfection will never be attained until Christ returns, I can see God conforming me daily to the image of Christ. Although I am not yet perfected, I am at least more aware of some of the areas of my life that need to be put to death daily.

For it became Him, for Whom are all things, and by Whom are all things, in bringing many sons unto glory, to make the Captain of their salvation perfect through sufferings.

Hebrews 2:10

CHAPTER 7

THE REWARDS OF SUFFERING

I do not claim to be perfect now and above committing any of these sins, but I have become very careful in my daily walk with God.

HEBREWS
CHAPTER 12:11

Now no chastening for the present seemeth to be joyous, but grievous: nevertheless, afterward it yieldeth the peaceable fruit of righteousness unto them which are exercised thereby.

THE rewards of suffering are priceless. They come only by the trial of faith through the fires of suffering.

SUFFERING DRAWS US CLOSER TO GOD. During my teenage years, I suffered tremendously from dysmenorrhoea (period pains). But remarkably, it was on those days when the pain was almost unbearable that I experienced God's presence more than at any other time. Not even in Church did I feel His presence so overwhelmingly. On those days, it felt like I could just reach out my hand and actually touch Him. Despite the pain, I used to bask in His presence. I felt so joyful, so peaceful, and so protected. I actually looked forward to having the pains, as any pain was worth the overwhelming presence of God that accompanied it.

We are drawn closer to the heart of God as our aching hearts keep in constant communication with Him, as we cry out for strength and relief.

God, in response, grants peace of mind and sends words of comfort, and we are thus strengthened. In thankfulness, we offer expressions of praise and worship to God. Until God delivers us from our afflictions, this constant communion continues and forms a bond which is not easily broken. A strong, intimate relationship between God and us is thus formed.

SUFFERING BRINGS SPIRITUAL GROWTH. Each time we are strengthened in our trials, there is growth. A firm foundation is built as we experience the goodness of God in the midst of our suffering. Our spiritual muscles are exercised as God stretches us and at the same time assures us that He is there with us no matter how painful the situation is and how hopeless it seems, and that He will cause all things to work together for our good.

SUFFERING PRODUCES RIGHTEOUSNESS, AS A RESULT OF ITS CHASTENING QUALITY. Righteousness has become the yearning of my heart. I have moved to a place of great carefulness where my thoughts, words, and deeds are under constant self-scrutiny and my desire is to live in the centre of God's will. If anything seems even remotely off course, I ask God to forgive and cleanse me and keep my hands clean and my heart pure.

Before this period of great anguish, such scrutiny and carefulness were never habitual. Sure, the sins that we label "big" were always obvious, and I knew I should avoid them. But what about the anger and bitterness I allowed to lay hold on me for so long before turning them over to God and allowing Him to help me to let go of them? And what about the malice, and the gossip, and the "little white lies," and the disunity, and the unkindness, and the consistent breaking of promises, and the little compromises, etc. that we sometimes allow to get a hold of us until we become so comfortable in them that they no longer appear to be sin? These are the "little" sins, in addition to the "big" sins, that I have become so careful about.

I do not claim to be perfect now and above committing any of these sins, but I have become very careful in my daily walk with God, and I strive to remain in the righteousness of Christ, and to walk in holiness, without which no man shall see the Lord (Hebrews 12:14).

Throughout the Word of God, we are instructed and warned to be vigilant in our walk with Christ, because our adversary, the devil, is like a roaring lion seeking whom he may devour (1 Peter 5:8). We cannot afford to drop our guard, because our enemy is a very crafty one, who constantly watches for an opportunity to strike and devour us. I remember so vividly that feeling of being swallowed by a snake that I experienced during the time I was trying so desperately to perceive God's forgiveness, and I indeed felt stolen, killed, and destroyed (St. John 10:10). 2 Corinthians 7:10-11 states, where sin, Godly sorrow and repentance are concerned: "*For Godly sorrow worketh repentance to salvation not to be repented of; but the sorrow of the world worketh death. For behold this selfsame thing, that ye sorrowed after a Godly sort, what* ***carefulness*** *is wrought in you, yea, what* ***clearing of yourselves****, yea, what* ***indignation****, yea, what* ***fear****, yea, what* ***vehement desire****, yea what* ***zeal****, yea what* ***revenge****! In all things, ye have approved yourselves to be clear in this matter.*"

I experienced the above scripture -- the Godly sorrow that worked repentance, the carefulness, the indignation (both Godly indignation for what I had done and shock that I had done it), the fear (both the fear of judgement and a greater fear of God), the vehement desire (in terms of striving for holiness) the zeal (for righteousness), the revenge (both in terms of wanting to hit back at the devil and what I wanted to do to make up for the wrong done), and the clearing of myself, in terms of the clearing of my conscience after repentance.

SUFFERING REVEALS GOD THROUGH EXPERIENTIAL KNOWLEDGE OF THE TRUTH OF HIS WORD IN A WAY THAT NOTHING ELSE CAN. In all the areas that I have gained deeper understanding of God, my knowledge of Him was formerly only superficial compared to the depth to which He revealed Himself through my suffering. A number of scriptures became experientially alive. Here are just a few examples:

"Now no chastening for the present seemeth to be joyous, but grievous: nevertheless, afterward it yieldeth the peaceable fruit of righteousness unto them which are exercised thereby." (Hebrews. 12:11)

"And He said unto me, My grace is sufficient for you, for My strength is made perfect in weakness." (2 Corinthians. 12:9)

"...I will never leave thee nor forsake thee." (Hebrews 13:5)

"...But where sin abounded, grace did much more abound:" (Romans 5:20)

"But the God of all grace, who hath called us unto His eternal glory by Christ Jesus, after that ye have suffered a while, make you perfect, stablish, strengthen, settle

you." (1 Peter 5:10)

SUFFERING MAKES US SENSITIVE TO AND UNDERSTANDING OF THE SUFFERING OF OTHERS. I avoided sharing my suffering with certain people because they did not understand what I was going through and thought I could just snap out of it or put it behind me and move on. Also, in some cases, people can be judgemental.

Please understand that we sometimes find ourselves in hardships that no power on earth can deliver us from. It is only the power of the **Almighty God** that can break some chains. I often said to God, "God, there are billions of people on this earth, but <u>not one single one</u> can help me; only You can." And I meant it. I could do nothing, but pray. No one else could do anything, but pray. As I have said before, I have come a long way, albeit with the help of people, but ultimately, it was the doing of the Almighty God, and the Almighty God alone!

Before this agonizing period of my life, I could NEVER understand what situation could be so bad in a person's life, that it could drive that person to even think about suicide, much less to commit the act. I do not have to wonder anymore; I have walked through that dark valley. I did not understand loneliness. All my life, I was just happy with myself. I enjoyed my own company, and being a part of the crowd was never my idea of fulfillment. I could be alone at anytime and I would be happy, fulfilled, and complete. My suffering brought me much loneliness, and then I understood what it was all about. Since then, loneliness for me has been the worst thing, next to depression.

SUFFERING PREPARES US TO HELP OTHERS WALK THROUGH THE VALLEY. When we have gone through and have been comforted by God, He prepares us to comfort others with the same comfort with which He comforted us (2 Corinthians 1:3-4). He equips us for use in the ministry of support and healing.

SUFFERING PREPARES US FOR MINISTRY. You would be surprised at the number of Christian ministries and the amount of literature and music that were conceived through the process of suffering. Our awesome God uses the process as a means of preparing us for great things. Suffering is a purifying tool which God uses to burn out all the impurities in us and conform us to the image of His Son, so that He can use us to accomplish His purposes and bring glory and honour to His name. We are kingdom builders, and one of God's training grounds is our suffering.

I have discovered that many authors have been born out of suffering, and I clearly understand why. Out of my pain, the thing I wanted to do most was write a book, because God inspired me to do so, as He revealed to me that so many people needed to know my story to help them through situations they are facing in their own lives, just as I needed to know other people's story to help me through my trials.

Another good thing that evolved from my experience is my appetite for reading. Before, I could never be considered an avid reader, but since, I have wanted to read every book that apply to my situation, and I have read several. You would never understand the tower of strength these books have been to me. That is one of the ways in which God uses our suffering to minister to the lives of countless others and bring comfort, hope, and healing to them.

But rejoice, inasmuch as ye are partakes of Christ's sufferings; that, when His glory shall be revealed, ye may be glad also with exceeding joy.

1 Peter 4:13

CHAPTER 8

CONFORMING TO HIS IMAGE

We can completely trust God with all things that concern us as He is perfecting them and causing them all to work together for our good.

ROMANS
CHAPTER 8:29

For whom He did foreknow, He also did predestinate to be conformed to the image of His Son, that He might be the firstborn among many brethren.

SUFFERING is a process of fiery trials and purification. I have learned that the refining process of silver and gold requires the refiner to sit facing the fire with the precious metal in the centre, which is the hottest part of the fire. As the metal is refined, the impurities surface and are removed. As long as impurities are found in the metal, the process continues, until all the impurities are burned out and removed. As long as the process lasts, the refiner sits there and keeps his eyes on the metal. He never leaves the metal in the fire unattended, as it could become over-processed and destroyed. How does the refiner know when the refining process is completed? When He sees a clear reflection of Himself in the refined metal.

Based on Malachi 3:3, the Lord shall sit as a refiner and purifier of silver. He sits as our refiner and purifier and He never leaves us or takes His eyes off us as long as we are in the refining process. This process continues until all the filth and dross are burned out of us and we come forth as pure gold in which He can clearly see His reflection. Thus, through the process of purification by fire He conforms us to His glorious image. I marvel at God's works! I just love His ways even though they are past finding out and we sometimes struggle to understand them and ask a lot of questions. His works sometimes are also very painful, but the reward is eternal glory, wrought through the fires of purification. We can completely trust God with all things that concern us as He is perfecting them and causing them all to work together for our good.

The following scriptures testify to our being conformed to Christ's image after purification by fire:

"Beloved, think it not strange concerning the fiery trials which is to try you, as though some strange thing happened unto you: But rejoice, in as much as ye are partakers of Christ's sufferings; that, when His glory shall be revealed, ye may be glad also with exceeding joy." (1 Peter 4:12)

..."That the trial of your faith, being much more precious than of gold that perisheth, though it be tried with fire, might be found unto praise and honour and glory at the appearing of Jesus Christ." (1 Peter 1:7)

"...if so be that we suffer with Him, that we may be also glorified together. For I reckon that the sufferings of this present time are not worthy to be compared with the glory which shall be revealed in us." (Romans 8:17-18)

"Forasmuch then as Christ hath suffered for us in the flesh, arm yourselves likewise with the same mind: for he that hath suffered in the flesh hath ceased from sin, that he no longer should live the rest of his time in the flesh to the lusts of men, but to the will of God." (1 Peter 4:1-2)

"But the God of all grace, who hath called us unto His eternal glory by Christ Jesus, after that ye have suffered a while, make you perfect, stablish, strengthen, settle you." (1 Peter 5:10)

Let us allow God to conform us to the image of His Son, though it be through the fires of suffering.

And be not conformed to this world: but be ye transformed by the renewing of your mind, that ye may prove what is that good, and acceptable, and perfect, will of God.

Romans 12:2

CHAPTER 9

I CANNOT FIND HIM

It is very helpful to know or to remember that ALL OF US at some time feel like God has hidden Himself from us.

JOB
CHAPTER 23:3

Oh that I knew where I might find Him! That I might come even unto His seat!

"OH, that I knew where I might find Him!" Are you at that place like Job, in a situation where you cannot find God? You go forward, but He is not there; and backward, but you cannot perceive Him. You go on the left hand, but you cannot behold Him; and He hideth Himself on the right hand, that you cannot see Him. (Job 23:8). That place of not being able to find God is indeed an extremely dark place, and while I was passing through, I felt like a wild, frightened animal; I felt completely lost and hopeless.

For those of you who are now going through that valley, have you read the book of Job and the Psalms recently? You will discover that these great men of God (Job, David, and other writers of the Psalms) also went through that valley of the shadow of death. You will discover that they never escaped the pains and afflictions of this life because they were such great men of God; you will discover that suffering is a common thread that runs through the entire human race, and you will find such hope, comfort, and strength in their experience with God as they walked through the valley. You will see how God delivered them, and be assured that He will also deliver you out of your afflictions with a mighty deliverance. Take a walk also through the books of Isaiah and Jeremiah; there you will find such wonderful promises and such words of comfort. You will also get to know God at a much deeper level.

It is very helpful to know or to remember that ALL OF US at some time *feel* like God has hidden Himself from us. This is a universal thing. Sometimes we cannot feel His presence; sometimes we are in big trouble and we seek Him and cannot seem to find Him. Sometimes our backs are against the wall and we call upon Him and we do not hear Him answer.

The circumstances in which He has seemingly forgotten us are many. But we must never fail to realize that God NEVER forgets us, and at those dormant times while we worry and fear and fret and sweat, He is quietly working in the background on our behalf.

I remember I was once in a job that I hated, and I kept talking to God about it -- nothing happened. My hatred for this job grew daily and I continued talking to God and -- nothing happened. One day I reminded

Him of the situation and told Him **I felt like He had forgotten me**. Immediately after that I took up my Bible and opened it right to Isaiah Chapter 49, and lo and behold, in verses 13-16, I read: *"Sing, O heavens; and be joyful, O earth; and break forth into singing, O mountains: for the Lord hath comforted His people, and will have mercy upon His afflicted. But Zion said, The Lord hath forsaken me, and my Lord hath forgotten me. Can a woman forget her suckling child, that she should not have compassion on the son of her womb? Yea they may forget, yet will I not forget thee. Behold, I have graven thee upon the palms of my hands; thy walls are continually before me."*

To the best of my memory, that was the first time God had ever spoken to me directly from His Word concerning a situation in my life. I have made it a habit to run to the Bible every time I have a pressing situation in my life, and it is amazing to see how God usually guides me directly to the scripture that addresses the problem or answers the questions that haunt me.

Another example is the night when I was so frustrated about my continual pain in relation to my broken marriage, my continual crying out to God to change the circumstances involved and heal the marriage, and

God's long delay in doing anything about it. I went to God whining and brooding, saying things like: "**God, look how long I have been hurting and suffering and putting up with this situation. I cry to You so much and it is like You are doing nothing about it. I am tired of it Lord. I am distressed, and I need Your guidance.**" I then shut up and opened my Bible right to St. Luke Chapter 18, where Jesus told a parable. He started the parable by saying *"...that men ought always to pray and not to faint"* and then He continued by telling about a widow who persistently bothered a judge for him to avenge her of her adversary. The judge did nothing to help her for a while, but eventually he could no longer deal with her bothering him, and so he avenged her of her enemy (end of parable). Jesus then went on to say: *"Hear what the unjust judge saith.* **And shall not God avenge His own elect, which cry day and night unto Him, though He bear long with them? I tell you that He will avenge them speedily..."**

Honestly, sometimes it is awesome that God should speak to me so clearly through His Word. Sometimes when this happens I just put the Bible aside and try to assimilate it. There was one case in point where I almost felt frightened at God's direct response. God has long been the excitement and joy of my life, and when I think that I can talk to Him so openly and hear from

Him so plainly, it is unspeakable.

Anyway, as far as the job mentioned above is concerned, it was just about two weeks after that answer from God that I found a new job, the best, not in terms of monetary reward, but in terms of job satisfaction, which was of far greater value to me. I saw the advertisement in the newspaper on Sunday, did an application letter on Wednesday, and delivered it personally. I was interviewed right there and then and given the job on the spot -- and I was given a ride by my prospective employer back to my present employer too, I might add.

Do you think that maybe St. Paul and his companions in Christ felt that same sense of being forgotten by God in 2 Corinthians 1:8, where, because of all the troubles they were facing, they despaired even of life? And what about David in Psalms 31, and 42, and 69 and …? Just read the Psalms. There you will find the writer saying he would have fainted if he had not expected to see the goodness of the Lord in the land of the living.

But St. Paul in verse 10 of 2 Corinthians 1 said that God delivered, and does deliver, and will yet deliver; and David has said to us over and over, trust in the Lord, be strong, be courageous, wait on the Lord … and God will deliver, God will deliver, God will deliver, God will deliver, God will deliver. Hello there! -- GOD ... WILL ... DELIVER!

That they should seek the Lord, if haply they might feel after Him, and find Him, though He be not far from every one of us. For in Him we live, and move, and have our being...

Acts 17:27

CHAPTER 10

THOUGH HE SLAY ME

The strangest thing in all this was that although sometimes it was so very difficult to trust God, trusting Him was really the ONLY thing I could do when my back was against the wall and I felt trapped between a rock and a hard place and had no idea what else to do.

PROVERBS
CHAPTER 3:5-6

Trust in the Lord with all thine heart and lean not unto thine own understanding.
In all thy ways acknowledge Him, and He shall direct thy paths.

FROM early in my walk with God, Job 13:15 became one of my favourite Bible verses, ***"Though He slay me, yet will I trust in Him."*** I knew then that I loved God, and the thought of loving Him so much that I would still trust in Him even though He slew me, was phenomenal. But that was how I felt about God. If you are a child of God, have you ever been so much in love with Him, and experienced His love flowing back to you so strongly, that you felt like you were His absolute favourite person? Of course you have! I believe we all experience this closeness and this sense of being so special to God at some point in our walk with Him. So, I was so much in love that He could slay me and I would just trust Him anyway.

Our trust in God is so very easy when life is well oiled and moving smoothly. If we encounter a little bump in the road and we are shaken a little, it is still fairly easy to maintain our trust in God. But when the boat has capsized, when the storm is raging and the waves are crashing over us, when tongues of fire lick us on every side, and when not only just the four walls are closing in on us, but also, the ceiling is descending and the floor is ascending, and when all of this seem to be happening at the same time, and we call out to God and we cannot see Him, hear Him, or feel Him, it is not that easy anymore. When this happens for an extended period of time, it makes it all the more difficult. People are known to have given up on God in such extreme circumstances.

My experience under those crushing circumstances was that my faith wavered so many times. So many times I felt like I had reached the breaking point and just could not go on any longer. So many times I wanted to give in to the enemy and just quit everything. So many times I did not have the strength or the will to live. So many times I felt that God had failed me and He was not going to deliver me. So many times I wondered if faith really worked and if God could really be trusted to change my situation. ***So many times I lost my faith and then God restored it.***

I never doubted that God had the power to deliver me from my distress, I just wondered whether He would do it for me. Yet, in all of this, God was so faithful. He knew my feeble frame and He knew my heart. Each time I was overwhelmed and my faith went wavering, I cried out to God and He restored me.

Even those times when I felt I could not trust God any more because the trials were too great and I did not see Him working on my behalf, He continued to supply and replenish. His grace was indeed sufficient for me and His strength was indeed made perfect in my weakness. He knew that deep down in my heart I did not want to give up on Him and that sometimes I had to will myself not to.

The strangest thing in all this was that although sometimes it was so very difficult to trust God, trusting Him was really the ONLY thing I could do when my back was against the wall and I felt trapped between a rock and a hard place and had no idea what else to do.

I will say of the Lord, He is my refuge and my fortress: my God; in Him will I trust.

Psalm 91:2

CHAPTER 11

I WILL NEVER LEAVE YOU

"God told me to tell you that you are special to Him and that you are the apple of His eye."

ST. MATTHEW
CHAPTER 28:20

Teaching them to observe all things whatsoever I have commanded you: and lo, I am with you always, even unto the end of the world. Amen.

DURING the many times when I could not "feel" God's presence, I believed that He had left me. This was so because never before had I been at a place where I could not feel His presence. But although this was the case, there were so many ways in which I could see His hand moving in my life. There were so many messages from Christendom that God seemed to have sent just for me.

The two common themes of all those messages were *God's forgiveness* even if I did not feel forgiven, and *God's presence* with me in the pit, in the valley, and in the dark places, and that He would deliver me in His time, after He had allowed the fiery trials to test me, purify me and make me as pure gold. Now, as I write this book, I can truly testify that indeed, He never left me nor forsook me. Even when I could not find Him or feel His presence, He was right there, bottling all my tears, sharing all my grief and pain, helping me to bear my heavy burden, and comforting me in so many different ways.

I would like to mention two instances in which God clearly assured me that He was with me. Earlier I mentioned my experience -- the Christian's experience -- of feeling very special to God. In the valley, I lost that feeling of being special. Sometime in June 2001, I shared with one of my sisters that once upon a time I used to feel so special to God, like I was the apple of His eye. I told her I did not feel that way anymore, and how much I longed to feel that way again.

One week after that, I was at a Church that I had visited a few times. I was feeling very depressed and very sick, and I rested my head on the back of the chair that was in front of me. A chorus was being sung, and a lady who was sitting in front of me came around and sat beside me. She held her head close to mine and sang the chorus to me, while she rubbed my back. When the chorus was finished, she said to me: "God told me to tell you that you are special to Him and that you are the apple of His eye, and **He is with you** no matter how bad the situation looks."

Wow! That was astounding! Do you see it? This woman and I were total strangers; I was only just visiting this Church. She knew nothing about me nor my circumstances. Just a week before I had shared with my sister that I used to feel special to God, like I was the apple of His eye but did not feel that way anymore.

Now this total stranger came to tell me God had told her to tell me **I was special to Him and I was the apple of His eye** and **He was with me no matter how bad the situation looked**. Wow!

In the second instance, when I was all messed up and was not functioning on the job, God moved on my behalf in so many little ways, but little ways which could have caused big embarrassment for me if He did not step in right in time and avert the mess I was about to make. He allowed me to make some mistakes, but divinely intervened and delivered me from the others right on the brink of messing up. This happened so often, and so often I would be saying, "Oh God, thank You, thank You, thank You…"

And, behold, I am with thee, and will keep thee in all places whither thou goest, and will bring thee again into this land; for I will not leave thee, until I have done that which I have spoken to thee of.

Genesis 28:15

CHAPTER 12

AMAZING GRACE

It was an awesome experience; an amazing grace!

2 CORINTHIANS CHAPTER 12:9

And He said unto me, My grace is sufficient for thee: for my strength is made perfect in weakness. Most gladly therefore will I rather glory in my infirmities, that the power of Christ may rest upon me.

ONE morning while I was sharing an apartment with a roommate, I walked into the kitchen where my roommate's household helper was preparing breakfast and said to her, "All your life you have been hearing about the grace of God; do you know what the grace of God is? Look at me, I am the grace of God." What I meant was that I was wrapped up in pure grace, as nothing but the grace of God could have kept me alive and going through the ordeal I was facing at the time.

I said that with a very strong conviction. I could never, ever have faced each day in my own strength. Without the grace of God, I would either have gone crazy or ended it all, as each day I felt like I was going crazy and I was bombarded by thoughts of death and suicide.

How could frail flesh and blood have withstood this? It could not. I was carried daily on the wings of God's grace. He was my daily strength. His grace guarded my heart and mind and His grace held me close to His heart and anchored me to the Rock, so I could NEVER do the things the enemy tempted me to do daily.

Another way in which I experienced the immeasurable grace of God in the most immense way was where I saw God take me from in terms of my struggle with believing He had forgiven me for the sin of adultery, and the place He brought me to in terms of ***knowing*** beyond the shadow of a doubt, that He had indeed forgiven me. I remember one day as I experienced this "knowing" in my spirit, I felt like I was the **only** person that existed, and the **only other thing** that existed with me was the vastness of God's grace, which appeared like a mist that filled the earth, with me standing exactly in the centre of it. This was more than just a feeling; it was like a real experience; a vision.

To get a good feel of this experience, picture yourself in a fog, where the only thing you can see is yourself. Now, picture that fog covering the **entire** earth with you, the only physical, tangible thing in existence, standing in the dead centre of it. The fog represented the grace of God, and I was engulfed by it.

It was an awesome experience; an amazing grace!

Let us therefore come boldly unto the throne of grace, that we may obtain mercy, and find grace to help in time of need.

Hebrews 4:16

CHAPTER 13

TRUSTING HIS PROMISES

How soon we tend to forget God's faithfulness and how weak our faith sometimes is.

NUMBERS
CHAPTER 23:19

God is not a man, that He should lie; neither the son of man, that He should repent: hath He said, and shall He not do it? or hath He spoken, and shall He not make it good?

THE PLANTED WORD

WHY do we sometimes find it so difficult to trust God, especially when He came through for us so many times before? Imagine getting a twofold promise from God, and to a great extent, seeing the first part of the promise being fulfilled in your life, but where the second part is concerned, everything seems to be going quite contrary to the promise. Where the second part is concerned, faith fluctuates based on the circumstances and the protracted period of time it seems to be taking God to fulfill that part of the promise. How soon we tend to forget God's ***faithfulness*** and how weak our faith sometimes is. Despite our frailty and our faithlessness, God remains faithful.

God planted a promise in my heart, and despite my wavering faith, I have never been able to put that promise out of my heart. In fact, countless days I have stood on that word for strength. I do not wish to go into the detail of the promise, except to say that it was given when I sought God back in 2000 concerning divorce. My conversation with God was something to this effect: "Lord, please tell me ***what to do*** **and** ***where to go*** concerning this matter." When I was finished, I opened my Bible directly to a chapter in Jeremiah, and started to read. As I read, I came to a particular verse in which some men were seeking direction from God, and it was quite striking to know that they, too, wanted God to ***"... show us the way wherein we may walk***, and ***the thing that we may do."*** God's response to their search for direction mirrored my situation, and I knew beyond doubt that God had clearly spoken to me.

THE WATERING OF THE WORD

It is absolutely amazing how God aids the trusting process. Remember, without God we can do nothing (St. John 15:5). We cannot even trust Him unless He helps us to do so. God has so watered the promise He planted in my heart as never before have I heard so many messages concerning holding on to the "promise" or the "word" or the "personal prophecy" given by God. These messages come from the Church in various meetings, they come from the pulpit of gospel television, and they come from gospel radio programmes -- all from people who don't even know I have a personal promise from God. After the messages started coming so consistently, I started referring to them as "the watering of the word" by God.

Interjection: Interestingly, just as I finished writing the last sentence above, I shifted my television channel to a Christian station just in time to hear a famous minister of the gospel say: "Whatever that promise is that God has given to you ... *hold on to it, never let it go."* She then continued by saying: **"It may be a promise concerning ..."** and her very next words were exactly what God had given me my promise about -- my marriage.

Do you see exactly what I mean when I say that God constantly waters the word -- the promise?

The word given by God and the watering of the word by God are quite sustaining. There have been so many times when I want to give up on the promise, but God's word cannot return unto Him void; it must accomplish what He sent it to accomplish (Isaiah 55:11). If you look at most other promises given to people in the Bible, you will notice that there is a great time period between the making of the promise and the fulfillment of the promise. After Abram received his promise of a son from God, it took well over ten years before the promise was fulfilled. We need to remember that God puts His timing to everything, and nothing will be accomplished before His timing. He tells us in His Word to *write the vision, and though it tarries, wait for it, because it will surely come, it will not tarry* (Habakkuk 2: 2-3).

For all the promises of God in Him are yea, and in Him Amen, unto the glory of God by us.

2 Corinthians 1:20

CHAPTER 14

HE LEADETH ME

Although I am still going through, the worst has passed, good has come, and the best is yet to come.

PSALM
CHAPTER 23:1-6

The Lord is my Shepherd; I shall not want. He maketh me to lie down in green pastures: He leadeth me beside the still waters.. He restoreth my soul: He leadeth me in the paths of righteousness for his name's sake. Yea, though I walk through the valley of the shadow of death, I will fear no evil: for Thou art with me; Thy rod and Thy staff they comfort me. Thou preparest a table before me in the presence of mine enemies: Thou anointest my head with oil; my cup runneth over. Surely goodness and mercy shall follow me all the days of my life: and I will dwell in the house of the Lord forever.

"HE LEADETH ME BESIDE THE STILL WATERS."

MY Storm has been raging. For over two years my lot in life was chronic depression, which generated fear, doubts, confusion, anxiety, irritability, mental dysfunction, insomnia, eating disorder, nervous conditions, job disruption, spiritual and emotional brokenness, and all the other conditions associated with chronic depression. At the time of writing, with less than one month to complete the third year since this all started, I can truly stand on the Word of God and proclaim that indeed many are the afflictions of the righteous, but the Lord delivers him out of them all (Psalm 34:19).

Although I am still going through, ***the worst has passed, good has come, and the best is yet to come.***

The waves are only now troubled; they are no longer raging and overwhelming me, and I have found rest to my soul.

"HE RESTORETH MY SOUL."

I lost a sense of His presence	-	*He restored it*
I lost my joy	-	*He restored it*
I lost my peace	-	*He restored it*
I lost my assurance	-	*He restored it*
I lost my hope	-	*He restored it*
I lost my purpose	-	*He restored it*
I lost my health	-	*He restored it*
I lost focus	-	*He restored it*
I lost mental clarity	-	*He restored it*
I almost lost my job	-	*He covered it*

God is a redeemer and a restorer. He can restore everything we have lost if we commit our ways to Him. What He requires of us above all things is obedience. When we walk in obedience, He can move mightily in our lives and accomplish through us all that He had designed for our lives from before the foundation of the world. Disobedience, on the other hand, can rob us in full or partial measure, of what God had ordained for us. TRUST God that the plan He has for your life is best, and OBEY Him in all He instructs you to do. Sometimes obedience brings pain, but I guarantee you that the pain of obedience will be glory compared to the pain that disobedience will surely bring.

"HE LEADETH ME IN THE PATHS OF RIGHTEOUSNESS."

In chapter 7, I mentioned the word "carefulness" and this is exactly what I have grown into over the past three years. As the Word of God says in 2 Corinthians 7:10-11, all this carefulness happens in the life of the Christian who falls in his walk with God. Before the fall, the walk is basically taken for granted and some amount of carelessness creeps in, but after the fall, vigilance and a deep hunger and thirst for righteousness, and living in the centre of God's will, forcefully become the blueprint for living.

To Him the porter openeth; and the sheep hear His voice: and He calleth His own sheep by name, and leadeth them out. And when He putteth forth His own sheep, He goeth before them, and the sheep follow Him: for they know His voice.

St. John 10:3-4

CHAPTER 15

I CAN DO ALL THINGS THROUGH CHRIST

I never thought I would have survived, but minute by minute, day by day, night by night, I endured the maddening pain and depression until God walked me right out of it, not in my strength, but in His.

PHILIPPIANS
CHAPTER 4:13

I can do all things through Christ which strengtheneth me.

DO you know it is really true? Well, it has to be; God said it.

In addition to the things revealed in this book, there were also other painful, untold events that I frequently had to deal with. I never dreamed I could deal with them, I never dreamed I could survive them, but I did, through Him who strengthened me. Even now, I am dealing with and doing things that could be considered "undoable," but I am doing them, through Him who strengthens me.

There is a telephone friend of mine (I have never met her – what a shame!), whom I used to talk with ever so often, and in every single conversation, she reminded me of this fact. My non-verbal response was always something like, "Sure, you can say anything, you are not the one who is suffering to the degree that I am suffering; you have no idea what I am going through." Her continuous reminder that I could do all things through Christ never brought me comfort. I could not even see that possibility.

Before I entered that period of my life, it was so believable. But now that I was at a place and time where I needed that head-knowledge and heart-belief to kick in and actually work for me, I lost faith in that divine word, because I was so blinded by my pain and everything that was happening in my life.

Now… ask me about it -- I went through it all. I never thought I would have survived, but minute by minute, day by day, night by night, I endured the maddening pain and depression until God walked me right out of it, not in my strength, but in His.

I have experiential knowledge of this word, and now I know that no matter what I face in this life, I can do all things through Christ who strengthens me.

But the salvation of the righteous is of the Lord: He is their strength in the time of trouble.

Psalm 37:39

CHAPTER 16

I DREAMED

Right then, the voice of God spoke to me (in the dream - I literally heard His voice like that of a man's) and said: "It is purpose, purpose, all purpose."

GENESIS
CHAPTER 40:8

And they said unto him, "We have dreamed a dream, and there is no interpreter of it." And Joseph said unto them, "Do not interpretations belong to God?...

Bitter-Sweet Dream

ONE night I dreamed I was by the Church where I got married and where my husband and I had attended for approximately ten years. There was something happening there; a function of some sort being held in the Church yard. Dreams have a way of exaggerating real life situations and in the dream I was feeling painfully lonely and debilitatingly depressed despite the movement of people and the buzz of activity all around me. My loneliness and depression were compounded by the fact that my matrimonial home was within walking distance of the Church (which is indeed so in reality), and I so had my mind on "home" and wanted to go there, but I could not, since I no longer belonged. In the dream, my emotional pain was immense, and despite the number of people around I never spoke with anyone.

In all that was happening, I looked around and saw a large waterfall, in the form of a basin-shaped rock, with the water flowing down on the inside of the basin, all around. As I continued to look at the flowing water, I realised that the *water itself* was actu*ally* my pain, my loneliness, and my depression. Right then, the voice of God spoke to me (in the dream - I literally heard His voice like that of a man's) and said: "It is purpose, purpose, all purpose."

I awakened from the dream.

From then on, I continued my walk through the valley of pain, loneliness, and depression knowing fully well that whatever God was leading me through, there was purpose to it and in the fullness of time He would reveal His purpose.

Sweet, Sweet Dream – A Child of The King

On another occasion I dreamed I was a princess. This dream was fairly short, and began with me being beautifully clothed in a long white dress and adorned with royal accessories, ascending the long flight of wide, slightly spiralled white steps that led to the beautiful, large white palace. As I entered the palace, I went to a table by which a handmaiden was standing, and she handed me something and said: "This is your special gift." The gift was packaged in burgundy and gold.

I awakened from the dream.

The gift that was contained in the package remains a mystery to this day, but I await the unwrapping of the package and the unravelling of the mystery.

But while he thought on these things, behold, the angel of the Lord appeared unto him in a dream, saying...

Matthew 1:20

CHAPTER 17

SOARING LIKE AN EAGLE

But in my state of deadness, LIFE spoke to me and gave me a promise which was far more glorious than the "ball of fire" in front of me – the promise of life, a hope and a future.

ISAIAH
CHAPTER 40:31

But they that wait upon the Lord shall renew their strength; they shall mount up with wings as eagles; they shall run, and not be weary; and they shall walk, and not faint.

THE title of this chapter depicts the way I feel and see myself after having gone through the brokenness and sin of my past. I knew where I was in Christ before I fell, and after falling, I thought I would never be able to find my position in Christ again. The enemy convinced me that I was undone, and would never be able to rise from my fall.

The enemy is a liar, and the father of lies; crafty and deceitful. He will use all his tools of deception to try to convince you to give up on God and to give up on yourself. He will try to get you to destroy yourself through his deception. He tries to keep you under this deception because he knows that if you can see beyond the lie, you will begin to rise. It is wonderful to know that where sin abounds, God's grace abounds much more.

I remember I visited my mother in St. Elizabeth about

a year ago. She had several plants of a beautiful flower in her garden, and I took a bulb of it back home with me and planted it. After a few days, the plant disappeared, and I could see no trace of it. I was so disappointed, because I thought it had died, and it was eventually forgotten.

One morning, after quite a long time had elapsed, I opened my front door and went onto the veranda, and lo and behold, there before me on the lawn, right at the very spot where I had planted that bulb, was the most beautiful sight. The plant had budded and flowered, apparently overnight, and was there like a beautiful ball of red fire, it all its glory.

Right then, in my messed up, painfully depressed, and seemingly hopeless state, the Holy Spirit spoke to my heart and told me that was a depiction of my life. He said that just like I thought that plant had died, and had now bloomed in all its glory, so would my life be. At the time, I mostly felt like a living body with a dead spirit -- a living dead, if you may. I merely existed; I never imagined that a living person could feel so dead in her spirit. But in my state of deadness, LIFE spoke to me and gave me a promise which was far more glorious than the "ball of fire" in front of me -- the promise of life, a hope and a future. Glory to God.

God can do wonders in all situations, and in my *hopefully-never-to-be-repeated* situation, He stretched me to the point where I know Him so much better and I can relate to His Word at such a deeper level. I understand His grace to such a limitless degree and I have seen that His faithfulness **never** lets go. I understand His ways so much better and my trust in Him has grown immensely. I have learned to handle the myriad difficulties of life so much more trustfully and restfully, and my desire for loving and serving God, for being in the centre of His will, and for walking in His righteousness, have blossomed and flourished. In short, I have grown in every respect. *I am learning* to view every other problem in my life against the backdrop of the agony I have suffered, and it makes everything so much lighter and so much more bearable. In the process, I waited on God, and He indeed caused me to mount up with wings as an eagle.

But Thou, O Lord, art a shield for me; my glory, and the lifter of my head.

Psalm 3:3

CHAPTER 18

ALL THINGS WORK... TO THEM THAT LOVE GOD

DO you get the picture?

ROMANS
CHAPTER 8:28

Now we know that all things work together for good to them that love God, to them who are the called according to His purpose.

DO you get the picture of how all things work together for good to them that love God, to them who are the called according to His purpose?

But as for you, ye thought evil against me; but God meant it unto good, to bring to pass, as it is this day, to save much people alive.

Genesis 50:20

CHAPTER 19

GREAT IS THY FAITHFULNESS

Nothing that happens in your life, not even falling into sin, is devoid of purpose; God salvages it and causes it all to work together for your good.

LAMENTATIONS
CHAPTER 3:22-23

It is of the Lord's mercies that we are not consumed, because His compassions fail not.
They are new every morning: great is Thy faithfulness.

IT is not only God's grace that is amazing; His faithfulness is too. In fact, everything about God is amazing. I am so glad that His name shall be called "Wonderful" (Isaiah 9:6). Sometimes when I cannot find the words to praise Him, I just say "You are so wonderful," and I get this deep sense of satisfaction that the name "Wonderful" covers it all. All His attributes are awe-inspiring. Oh, the depth of God's ***faithfulness***! Oh, the depth of all His attributes! They are past finding out. Our human minds cannot fathom them; they are too limitless for us to grasp them.

When my human mind comprehended God's grace in the context of me being the only person in the world and the only other thing that existed with me was the grace of God that filled the universe with me standing in the centre of it (Chapter 12), that was only just a fraction of His grace that I experienced, because the mere fact that my mind could grasp it proves that it was only just a drop in the bucket. All God's attributes are as everlasting as He is, and He is from everlasting to everlasting (Psalm 90:2), being the same yesterday, today and forever (Hebrews 13:8). Now, try to grasp that!

Herein lies God's ***faithfulness***: (1) He gives you a word. (2) He honours His word above His name. (3) He says, "I will never leave you nor forsake you." (4) No matter where life leads you, God is already there. (5) Even when you cannot feel His presence, He is there. (6) When you fall, He will lift you up. (7) When you walk out on Him, if it were left up to you, you would not return; it is He who draws you back to Him. (8) Nothing that happens in your life, not even falling into sin, is devoid of purpose; God salvages it and causes it all to work together for your good.

Have you ever felt like the prodigal son, unworthy to be called a child of God and unworthy of all the goodness He lavishes upon you after you vacationed with the pigs and returned home? I have felt like the prodigal son, -- very unworthy. Nevertheless, I still wanted to do something for God, but all I felt worthy of doing was sweeping the Church, nothing more. I remember one day saying to a friend "Only just to sweep the Church." We had both been in the pigpen, and she felt the same sense of unworthiness and thought also of "only just sitting at the back of the

Church or cleaning the Church." At this point in my life, I still feel like the prodigal son, but in his exalted position. The first part of the promise I got from God was that if I did what He required me to do, He would build and plant me, and I have watched in amazement as He fulfills this promise.

Earlier I touched on the matter of obedience. Do not miss this point -- when God gave me the promise, He said that if I would do a certain thing, then He would build me and not pull me down, and He would plant me and not pluck me up. I have done what God required, and He has been fulfilling His promise. Be sure that if I did not carry out His requirement, I would be one of the most miserable souls today, without a hope of receiving the promise. ***The process of building and planting continues.***

Herein again lies God's *faithfulness*: If your failure to keep your side of a covenant with God causes you to lose out on what He had promised, you will no doubt pay a painful price, but in the end, God's *faithfulness* will prevail, because He will find a way to redeem you from yourself and to use the pit you put yourself into to work for your good. Get this: God ***always*** causes us to triumph in Christ (2 Corinthians 2:14). If we do not believe, He abides faithful: He cannot deny Himself (2

Timothy 2:13).

God's people are the Church, and in the end, the Church triumphant is alive and well.

GREAT Is Thy *Faithfulness*!

I will sing of the mercies of the Lord for ever: with my mouth will I make known Thy faithfulness to all generations. For I have said, Mercy shall be built up for ever: Thy faithfulness shalt Thou establish in the very heavens. I have made a covenant with my chosen, I have sworn unto David my servant, Thy seed will I establish for ever, and build up thy throne to all generations. And the heavens shall praise Thy wonders, O Lord, Thy faithfulness also in the congregation of the saints. For who in the heaven can be compared unto the Lord? Who among the sons of the mighty can be likened unto the Lord. God is greatly to be feared in the assembly of the saints, and to be had in reverence of all them that are about Him. O Lord God of hosts, who is a strong Lord like unto Thee? Or to Thy faithfulness round about Thee?

Psalm 89: 1-8

CONCLUSION

A great price has been paid for the writing of this book. The total cost is found in the contents of the book. I believe God wanted this book written, but He knew it would never have been possible if He did not allow me to experience a little hell on earth. This book was not written for my glorification; it was written for everyone of like suffering, **WHATEVER** the cause, and ultimately for the glory of God.

People of like suffering include everyone who, because of the great agony with which they are living, believe that their suffering is exceedingly, abundantly, and above everyone else's suffering; that their life is over, that things will NEVER change, that God has forsaken and forgotten them, that He can never forgive them for that horrible sin they have committed, that they cannot bear it for one second longer, that they will die in the process, that they want to commit suicide and end it all, that the situation is hopeless, hopeless, hopeless. This is the meaning of depression. It is not the end of the world; it is just depression of the highest order, and this too, will pass, if you allow God into your circumstances.

I have gone through all of the above, and I live today to

testify of the power, the goodness, the grace, the love, and the faithfulness of THE LORD GOD ALMIGHTY in WHATEVER circumstances we face today. Trust me … when I tell you that I SUFFERED and I believed that my situation was the greatest evil to ever befall anyone, and it was so dark and hopeless that I just wanted to die, I mean it with all my being. When I see where I am today, I knew I had to tell as many persons as I could reach that God is, God is, God is -- EVERYTHING you need Him to be and EVERYTHING He has promised to be. God is SO FAITHFUL, God is SO PRESENT, and if you would only just put ALL your trust in Him and GIVE HIM TIME to work through your circumstances, there is ABSOLUTELY NO SITUATION He cannot deliver you from.

It is very important for you to know that TIMING in God's economy is of the highest importance. We dwell in time; God dwells in eternity. We are ALWAYS in a hurry; God is NEVER in a hurry. A day with Him is like a thousand years, and a thousand years is like a day (2 Peter 3:8). If we patiently wait on God and not give up on Him, He will come through for us, every time. Many people have committed suicide, and they would be stars today if they had trusted God and patiently waited on Him. The Word of God Says: "**…But they** that wait upon the Lord shall renew their strength; they shall mount up with wings as eagles; they shall run, and not be weary; and they shall walk, and not faint." **(Isaiah 40:31).** WHATEVER you are going through, God's word to you is, **"Behold, I will do a new thing; now it shall spring forth; shall ye not know it? I will even make a way in the wilderness, and rivers in the desert." (Isaiah 43:19).**

There is a proverb that says time heals all wounds. I submit to you that it is not time that heals; it is God who heals -- time is His medicine.

Again, it is important to know what waiting on God means. It means working and being active, as hard as that may be, and trust me, I know how hard it can be. The times when I wanted to quit was when everything was just so hard to do and I just did not have the strength to do it, but God enabled me. Waiting means crying out to God and trusting Him with your circumstances, knowing that at all times He knows best and He knows just how to deal with the problem, in His time. Waiting means you do not go overboard in trying to fix the problem yourself, because most times all we do is make things worse; you do not seek to take revenge, because this further messes up everything and takes God's blessings away. The Lord says the battle is not yours, it is His (2 Chronicles 20:15/17), and He says that vengeance is His, He will repay (Romans 12:19). Waiting means reading, standing, and leaning on the Word of God. His Word was my strong and mighty tower. I ran to it so often when I wanted to give up and each time I was fortified and strengthened and given the will to go on.

Sometimes we do things that bring agonizing situations into our lives. One very powerful, special, comforting, and strengthening verse I found while I immersed myself in the Word of God was ***"O Israel, thou hast destroyed thyself; but in Me is thine help."*** (Hosea 13:9).

No matter what situation we face in life, in God is our help, and He will work all things together for our good. Wait upon Him and allow Him to bring these promises to pass in your life.

I believe it is instructive at this point to say, never be fooled by yourself or anyone else that depression is a condition that the sufferer can snap himself or herself out of. It is not a condition that one gets into or out of voluntarily. It is a terrible, terrible, terrible, too-deep-to-be-described; I-would-rather-die-than-live mental condition. While I would like for you to understand this condition to the point where you do not misguidedly judge people you may know suffering from the condition, I would never like for you to gain that understanding from personal experience. The resources for research are many; some of them right at your fingertips, if you are so inclined.

Summary

Just in case the crucial points I tried to convey got lost somewhere in the details of the book, I summarize them below:

You Are Forgiven

Never doubt God's forgiveness -- you are forgiven. If you cannot feel His presence -- you are forgiven. If you cannot feel a sense of being forgiven, keep on holding on -- you are forgiven. If your joy is totally gone -- you are forgiven. No matter what, as long as you ask for His forgiveness -- *you are forgiven.*

You Must Go Through

You must go through WHATEVER you are going through. It is not that God does not love you; it is that He loves you. It is not that God has forgotten you; it is that He remembers you. You must be purified, you must be made fit for the Master's use, you must be strong, your faith must be unwavering, you must conform to the image of Christ, you must know God at a much deeper level; and the fiery trials is the means by which God accomplishes all this in your life. The fiery trials must come; just stand fast and allow God to do the work He needs to do in you.

It Is A Lie

It is all right to feel like this agony will never end, but never, never believe that lie. That lie could cost you your life and your soul.

In Every Situation

God has the power to deliver from any and every excruciating situation. There is always purpose in the times when He allows us to suffer beyond what it seems we can bear. Our part is twofold: (1) to seek Him and trust Him (He has promised we will find Him if we seek Him with all our heart, and He has said that we should acknowledge Him in all our ways and He will direct our path); and (2) use all the legitimate resources He has made available to us to effect our recovery. Do not forget that everything is by Him, including the resources He made available, and without Him is nothing made, that was made.

GENERAL OBSERVATIONS AND ENCOURAGEMENT

- I have observed that everything we experience in life is common to mankind. Countless number of people are going through exactly what you are going through. As difficult as this may be to believe, it is true. This discovery helped me to cope much better with my affliction and it played a major role in my own healing.

- When we go through extremely adverse situations, we are inclined to stay away from the house of God. The person who is suffering from clinical/chronic depression just wants to curl up in bed and die. It is the hardest thing to get out of bed to go anywhere. If we succumb to this tendency to curl up and die, we aggravate the problem. The fastest route out is to get active, as "impossible" as that might be. The most therapeutic activity is to find ourselves in the house of God, where the spirit will be lifted by the praise and worship and the Word of God.

- Do not expect immediate healing; healing and restoration comes gradually. However, each time we enter God's presence to worship with His people, our spirit gets stronger until it begins to rise above the depression. Force yourself to the house of God if you have to. For almost two years into my depression I had to force myself to go to Church. It did not come naturally anymore, and quite often it was the last thing I wanted to do. Frequently the depression rested heavily on me throughout the service, but even during those times the Spirit of God administered healing to me as hope would rise amidst the greatest despair, and with hope came joy. Little, by little, by little, by little, on a weekly basis, this happened, and now, my joy has returned and I go to the house of God excitedly and expectantly each week.

The presence and the Word of God bring healing -- do not neglect so great a salvation.

SPECIAL NOTE

I would never like to go through another trial as intense as this one, but looking back over the past three years, looking at where I am now, and looking down into the future, I am extremely happy that God allowed me to have had the experience. Already, I am better for it, and so much more good is yet to come.

Amen!

My Tribute To God

"YOU"

Sometimes I rack my brain just trying to find the most impressive words to tell You. And what do I want to tell You? I want to tell You how I feel about You. I want to tell You how much I love You, but just saying that does not seem to adequately say it.

I want to tell You how good, and how great, and how awesome, and how perfect, and how mighty, and how wonderful, and how beautiful, and how faithful, and how merciful, and how holy, and how righteous... You are, but all that don't seem to adequately say it.

You are so much more than all the above. I think I might need to expand my vocabulary, but then, I really don't think that will help, because my spirit tells me that I could study the biggest volume and still not find words adequate to express my praise of You.

Sometimes when my heart yearns to praise You

because of all the joy and love I feel for You, and my human words are not sufficient to express myself to You, I just break down and weep before You.

How can I adequately praise the God who is the Creator and sustainer of this vast and awesome universe, and everything that is in it? -- the God who is from everlasting to everlasting? -- the God who has no beginning and no end? -- the God who is everywhere at all times, from whose presence we cannot hide? -- the God who is all-powerful, with whom nothing is impossible? -- the God who is all seeing, beholding all things at all times and knowing the thoughts and intent of every heart? -- the God who knew us from before the very foundation of the world? -- the God who knows our ending from our beginning? -- the God who holds our times in His hands? -- the God who numbers every hair on our heads and writes all our members in a book? -- the God who is so much more than all that? -- and yet the Great and Mighty God who loved us so much that He took on humanity and gave His life for us who were dead in trespasses and sin, so that we might have eternal life and reign with Him forever?

TEACH ME HOW TO PRAISE YOU.

ABOUT THE AUTHOR

The fourth day of the week, fourth day of the month, fourth month of the year was the clash of the fours that heralded the birth of Lurline Ebanks in 1962, in the district of Flagaman, St. Elizabeth, Jamaica. She is the last of eight children.

Lurline migrated to Kingston, Jamaica, at age 14 to live with her sister and continue her schooling. She attained the qualification of Certified Professional Secretary and currently works in that profession. In December 2007 she completed a course of studies which will lead to the award of an Associate Degree in Business Administration, and she is currently pursuing a Bachelor's Degree in Human Resource Management.

She was born again at age 17, when God sweetly and powerfully "invaded" her life in the shower at Ocean View Bible Camp in St. Elizabeth. This "invasion" of her life is a simple but amazing example of how God sets the stage when He wants to make a move in our lives. Every evening at camp several persons would be in the bathroom at the same time using the various shower compartments, dressing the hair, brushing the teeth, or performing some other activity. As God would have it, quite uncharacteristically Lurline was the only person in the entire bathroom on this particular evening having a shower, with God being the last person on her mind even though she was on holy grounds. ***Suddenly***, she was overwhelmed by a joy that was so intense that she started to cry, dance, clap, sing, and praise God -- all at once. She knew then, beyond the shadow of a doubt, that she had been born again -- and her life has been changed forever.

Upon migrating to Kingston, she went to live immediately next door to her future husband, and this was how they met. They got married on September 26, 1987, and on August 18, 1992, Lurline became Mother to a beautiful baby girl.

She has been involved in various Church ministries over the years, including the Music Ministry (as a choir member - her first love), Young Peoples Ministry, Altar Workers Ministry, Evangelism Ministry, and Prison Ministry.

She is presently a Member of Church on the Rock, Kingston, Jamaica.

LIST OF REFERENCED BIBLE VERSES

Isaiah 59:1-2
Philippians 3:10
Romans 8:29
2 Corinthians 12:9
Romans 8:28
Isaiah 55:9
St. John 10:10
1 Peter 5:10
1 Peter 4:12
1 Peter 4:1-2
St. John 15:5
Isaiah 9:6
2 Timothy 2:13
2 Chronicles 20:15/17
St. Matthew 27:46
1 Peter 5:6
Job 23:3
Numbers 23:19
Lamentations 3:22-23
Romans 11:33
2 Corinthians 7:10-11
2 Corinthians 1:3-4
1 Peter 4:1-2
St. John 15:5
Isaiah 9:6
2 Timothy 2:13
Romans 12:19
2 Timothy 1:12
James 1:22-25
Proverbs 3:5-6
Psalm 23:1-6
Acts 9:5
Hebrews 12:14
Hebrews 13:5
1 Peter 4:12
Job 23:8
Isaiah 55:11
Psalm 90:2
2 Peter 3:8
Hosea 13:9
Job 40: 1-8
Hebrews 2:11
St. Matthew 28:20
Isaiah 40:31
St. John 11:25
1 Peter 5:8
Romans 5:20
1 Peter 1:7
Isaiah 49
Habakkuk 2:2-3
Hebrews 13:8
Isaiah 43:19
Philippians 4:13
Genesis 40:8

Note: Footnote scriptures excluded

Update

This update was made in December 2007, shortly before publication of this book.

Up to December 2005 I still struggled with occasional bouts of pain and depression, resulting from various encounters with my husband. The pain of each encounter would cut so deeply I would plunge right back into depression, but I would recover from these bouts of depression in a very short period of time. It was this situation that eventually drove me to start divorce proceedings. Not that I wanted to do so, but I could feel myself being propelled to take this step by each emotional blow. The proceedings were put on hold once, taken off hold, and then eventually cancelled.

Although my husband and I are still separated, I am now totally beyond all the pain and all the depression -- but how the loneliness lingers…

As I proofread this page, it is 1:27 A.M. on December 25, 2007, and I am absolutely happy just listening to Christmas carols on the radio. Christmas is my absolute favourite time of the year, and I remember prior to going into depression I always said over the years that nothing could ever happen to spoil Christmas for me. The depression robbed me of Christmas 2000, 2001, and 2002.

notes

notes

www.ingramcontent.com/pod-product-compliance
Ingram Content Group UK Ltd.
Pitfield, Milton Keynes, MK11 3LW, UK
UKHW041846190726
13854UKWH00002B/748

9 781425 165819